First published in Great Britain in 2025 by Hodder & Stoughton
© Hodder & Stoughton Ltd 2025
All rights reserved
Managing editor: Victoria Brooker / Design: Ellie Boultwood
ISBN: 9781445191539 (hbk) / ISBN: 9781445191553 (pbk) / ISBN: 9781445191546 (ebk)

Franklin Watts, an imprint of Hachette Children's Group
Part of Hodder & Stoughton
Carmelite House, 50 Victoria Embankment, London EC4Y 0DZ

An Hachette UK Company

www.hachette.co.uk
www.hachettechildrens.co.uk

Printed and bound in Dubai

The authorised representative in the EEA is Hachette Ireland, 8 Castlecourt Centre, Dublin 15, D15 XTP3, Ireland (email: info@hbgi.ie)

CoNTENTS!

4	GET	Communicating!
6	GET	Speaking!
8	GET	Talking!
10	GET	Moving!
12	GET	In Touch!
14	GET	Wagging!
16	GET	Carving!
18	GET	Writing!
20	GET	Spelling!
22	GET	Scrolling!
24	GET	Printing!
26	GET	Signalling!
28	GET	Inventing!
30	GET	Broadcasting!
32	GET	Into Space!
34	GET	Online!
36	GET	Sharing!
38	GET	Conversing!
40	GET	Chatting!
42	GET	Speaking Out!
44	GET	Connected!
46		Glossary
47		Further Information
48		Index

Get Communicating!

Communication is when information, thoughts and feelings are shared. It's unbelievably important. Without it, we wouldn't be able to make friends. We'd find it difficult to explain how we really feel. And we'd have no idea what anyone else thought about **ANYTHING**.

We communicate by speaking, by using expressions and gestures, by writing words and by using images. Here are some examples ...

FIVE WAYS OF COMMUNICATING

USING A LOUDSPEAKER
to direct a crowd of people AT TOP VOLUME

SMILING
to show someone that you're happy

SENDING A FUNNY CARD
to make someone laugh

READING THE NEWS ON TELEVISION
to explain to everyone what's going on

WRITING SONG LYRICS
to tell a love story

TRUE OR FALSE?

During a conversation, only the speaker is communicating.

FALSE!

It takes at least two people for communication to happen – one person to share something and another to receive it. If one person is speaking and no one is listening to them, then absolutely nothing is being communicated.

Communication isn't just sharing important facts or letting someone know what you think. It's a great way to **CONNECT** with others, too. Sometimes, it doesn't even matter what you're saying – just getting in touch shows the other person that you've thought of them!

DID YOU KNOW...?

Over **eight trillion** text messages are sent each year. That's over 20 billion every single day!

In actual numbers, that's more than 8,000,000,000,000!

How many different ways of communicating can YOU think of?

GEt SpEAkINg!

Human speech might have been around for two million years! Scientists think that **EARLY HUMANS** may have used a form of speech to teach others how to make tools. But as sounds obviously vanish as soon as they are spoken, no one knows for sure. As well as being one of the oldest types of communication in the world, speech is one of the easiest, too. There's no special equipment required. All you need to chat, whisper, discuss, announce and SHOUT is ... you.

Homo habilis – wh[ich] means 'handy ma[n]' had a larger brain t[han] earlier human spec[ies]

TRUE OR FALSE?

It takes one sixth of the muscles in the human body to speak.

TRUE!

Of the 600 muscles in your entire body, you use about 100 of them to speak! These muscles aren't all in your tongue; they're also in your lips, face, jaw, neck and chest.

EIGHT PARTS OF THE BODY WE USE TO SPEAK

LUNGS – these release a stream of air that's used to create sound

LARYNX – this is another name for the voice box, where sound is made

VOCAL CORDS – these folds of stretchy tissue in your voice box vibrate when air travels through them

TONGUE – by moving your tongue, you can form many sounds, such as D, L, N, S, T and Z

LIPS – putting these together creates the sounds B, M and P

TEETH – these are used to make the sounds F, TH and V

MOUTH and NOSE – air travels out of these to make sounds and words

Get Talking!

Over 6,000 languages are spoken in the world today!

LANGUAGES are collections of sounds that we use to communicate with others. Each language has its own words and rules, so that its speakers know how to use it.

No one knows for sure why we have different languages. They may all be descended from one original language. Or languages may have developed independently around the world.

THREE SURPRISING SOUNDS USED TO TALK

HUMMING
the Pirahã people in the Amazon rainforest

WHISTLING
the Hmong people of South-east Asia

CLICKING
Khoisan languages spoken in parts of Africa

TRUE OR FALSE?

The famous playwright William Shakespeare invented 1,700 words.

TRUE!

If there wasn't a word in the English language to describe exactly what Shakespeare meant, he simply invented a new one. In fact, he invented over 1,700 of them, including: bedroom, eyeball, fashionable, gossip, luggage, puking and zany. Shakespeare came up with phrases too. 'Wild-goose chase' – meaning a hunt for something that is ridiculous and pointless – first appeared in the play *Romeo and Juliet*.

DID YOU KNOW...?

Papua New Guinea is an island country north of Australia. Here, more languages are spoken than in any other country in the world – **over 800** of them!

The world's most spoken language is English. But Mandarin Chinese is the most popular **first** language – the language a person learns to speak first of all.

GET MOVING!

We don't just use words to communicate. We also use a huge variety of gestures, expressions and movements to add meaning to what we say. This type of communication is known as **BODY LANGUAGE.**

It's called non-verbal communication, too. That's because there are no words!

FIVE TYPES OF BODY LANGUAGE

FROWNING
This can show that someone is angry or disapproving or doesn't understand.

OPENING EYES WIDE
If someone does this, they might be astonished, shocked or delighted.

RUBBING THEIR CHIN
Someone might be thoughtful or disbelieving or trying to solve a problem.

SHRUGGING
This can show that someone is clueless, that they have no idea about something or they just don't care.

SMILING
This is the perfect way for someone to show that they are pleased, proud or thrilled.

Pick any phrase and say it in a cheery way. Then say it in the most sarcastic voice ever to change the meaning!

Body language can add a lot to a conversation. An expression or a gesture can show a whole range of emotions. Meanwhile, the way in which we speak is filled with meaning. Your tone can show that you really mean what you say or that you mean totally the opposite.

TRUE OR FALSE?

Speech is always spoken. The only way of having a conversation with someone is by speaking.

FALSE!

Sign language is a way for deaf people to speak and listen without sound. Hands, expressions and body movements are used to communicate with others instead. There are over three hundred different sign languages around the world!

GET IN TOUCH!

Our senses of sight, hearing and touch help us to communicate. But for some, the sense of touch is especially important. **TACTILE** signing is a way of communicating using touch. It allows deafblind people to connect with others. It means that those with hearing loss can connect with people with sight loss, too.

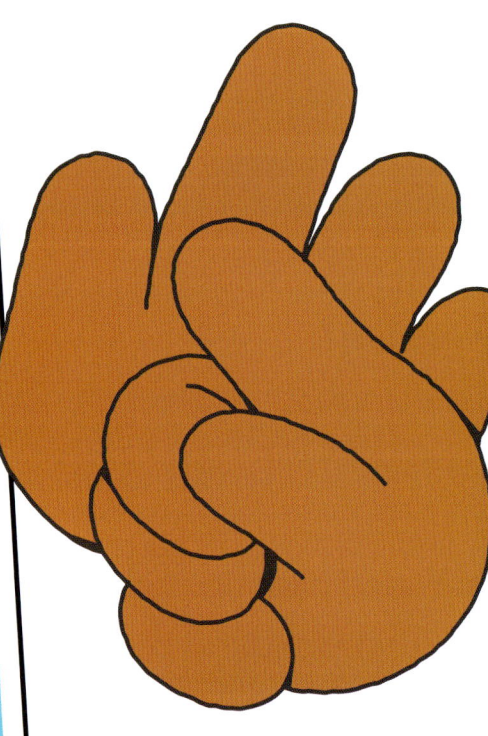

TWO WAYS OF TACTILE SIGNING

DEAFBLIND MANUAL
Letters are signed one by one onto the palm of someone's hand, so words can be spelt out. It's based on a sign-language alphabet.

HAND-OVER-HAND
The person who's receiving the message puts their hands on top of the hands of the person sending the message.

DID YOU KNOW...?

Helen Keller, who was born in 1880 in Alabama, USA, was **deafblind.** Helen famously learnt how to read Braille (see page 25), use sign language and to speak.

Among Helen's many **achievements**, she graduated from university, was awarded the Presidential Medal of Freedom and was elected to the National Women's Hall of Fame in New York City, USA.

TRUE OR FALSE?

A sixth sense exists.

TRUE!

Many people believe they have a sixth sense that warns them of approaching disaster. But your sixth sense is actually something very different. It's called proprioception and tells you where your body is and what your joints and limbs are doing – without having to look for them. (So, unfortunately, your sixth sense won't tell you the right answers in a test. You'll still have to revise for that.)

GET WAGGING!

It's only in books, cartoons and films that animals speak like humans. But you might be surprised to learn that **ANIMALS** communicate in other surprising ways in real life.

FIVE TYPES OF ANIMAL COMMUNICATION

WAGGING
Dogs use their tails to show their emotions; a big, sweeping wag means that a dog is happy.

SINGING
Whales use their vocal cords to produce different notes; when put together, these make a whale song!

DANCING
Bees dance to tell other bees that they've found food.

FANNING
A peacock displays his colourful tail to attract a mate.

GROOMING
Monkeys pick ticks and lice from each other's fur to show affection.

Animals of the same species communicate with each other to send and receive information. This might be to tell another animal that they are in charge, to warn of danger, to attract a mate or to take care of young.

TRUE OR FALSE?

Cats only miaow when they speak to humans.

TRUE!

Kittens miaow to tell their mothers that they're hungry. But once they've grown up, they stop miaowing at other cats. They do, however, miaow at humans. This may be to ask someone to feed them, let them out of the house or to stroke them.

DID YOU KNOW...?

Like babies, **dogs** pay attention to the way that people speak and **recognise** when a human is talking to them.

In fact, scientists think that dogs are as good as **six-month-old babies** at understanding what people mean!

GET CARVING!

Speaking is an excellent way of communicating, but the problem with the spoken word is that it doesn't last. Long ago, rock art meant that people could **RECORD** their stories on rock surfaces for others and for future generations.

TWO TYPES OF ROCK ART

PETROGLYPHS
These are made by carving, chipping or scratching away the surface of rock. Some images have been discovered that date back 12,000 years!

PICTOGRAPHS
Made by painting onto rock, this art is easily worn away by rain, wind and sun. But ancient examples have been found in rock caves, safe from the weather!

The ancient Egyptians' rock carvings weren't just pictures. Their hieroglyphs were symbols of people, animals and things, such as two reeds, a lion and a horned viper. But although some hieroglyphs represented the objects they showed, they usually stood for a sound. When put together, these sounds made words.

TRUE OR FALSE?

In ancient Egypt, everyone understood hieroglyphics.

FALSE!

Hardly any ancient Egyptians knew how to read – never mind write – hieroglyphics. Historians think that it was just a few priests who knew what they meant! Hieroglyphics stopped being used altogether around 400 CE. Soon, there was no one left who could understand them and hieroglyphics became a code for historians to crack!

Justimaginereadingasentencewheretherearenospacesbetweentheletters!

DID YOU KNOW...?

There is absolutely no punctuation whatsoever in hieroglyphic writing. There aren't even any spaces!

GET WRITING!

There are about 300 writing systems around the world, including the one in this book! **CUNEIFORM** is probably the oldest writing system ever. It was invented over 5,000 years ago by the Sumerians, in the country that's now Iraq.

Cuneiform means 'wedge-shaped'.

Writing cuneiform meant pressing the end of a reed into squidgy clay to form tiny wedge-shaped marks. These were used to make hundreds of unique characters, which each represented a sound. When the characters were put together, they created words!

The Sumerians also invented seconds, minutes and hours!

SOME OF THE GAZILLION PLACES YOU'LL FIND WRITING

- In bestselling books
- On signs above a motorway
- In a recipe for how to make chocolate eclairs
- On a website selling school uniforms
- Iced onto birthday cakes
- On packets of spaghetti
- Inside a secret diary
- In the sky – on a banner pulled by an aeroplane!

TRUE OR FALSE?

The Rosetta Stone was a codebreaking device.

(SORT OF) TRUE!

The Rosetta Stone was inscribed in 196 BCE with the same text, in three different languages: ancient Egyptian hieroglyphics, Demotic script and ancient Greek. When the ancient stone was discovered in Egypt in 1799, language experts were able to compare the different writing systems. Finally, they were able to start working out what the hieroglyphs actually meant!

GET SPELLING!

Hundreds of writing systems are used today. Each uses letters or characters that provide the building blocks for languages around the world. Here are some of the most popular.

The **LATIN ALPHABET** uses 26 letters to represent sounds. English, French, Italian and Norwegian are just a few of the languages that use it to write.

There are thousands of **CHINESE CHARACTERS** and every one of them represents a word! They are used to write Mandarin, Japanese, Korean and Vietnamese.

DEVANĀGARĪ has 48 letters. It's easy to recognise because of the horizontal line at the top of each letter; when a word is written, these join up to form a continuous line.

The **ARABIC ALPHABET** has 28 letters, which are all consonants. This script is used in Farsi, Urdu and Kurdish and is written from right to left.

20

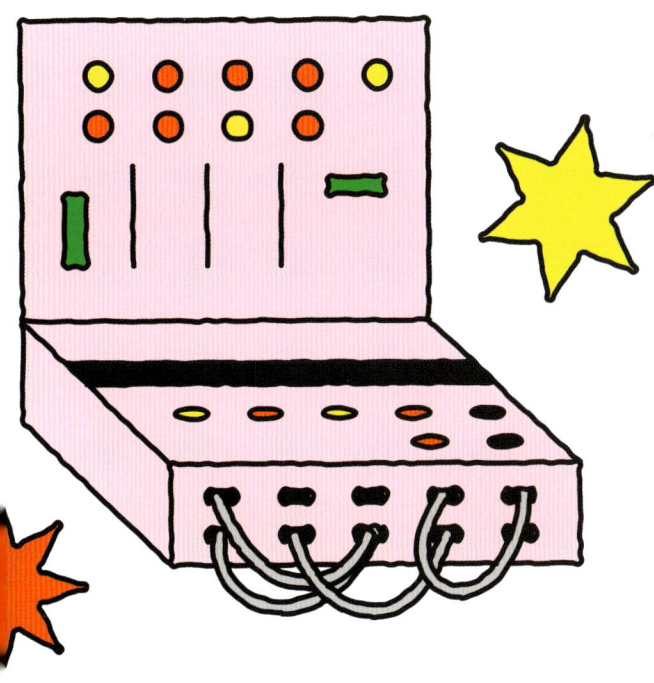

TRUE OR FALSE?

The Enigma machine was a fancy typewriter.

FALSE!

It might have looked like a typewriter, but the Enigma machine was actually a German coding device. It was used to disguise important messages during the Second World War (1939–45). But when Polish and British codebreakers discovered how Enigma worked, they were able to decipher messages and discover their enemy's secret plans!

ç   ñ

ø

DID YOU KNOW...?
The dots, marks, lines and wiggles that appear above, below or strike right through letters in some languages are called **diacritics**!

ç

é

They often tell us how the letter is **pronounced**. But, in some languages they stand for **vowel** sounds.

ø   ñ

é

Get Scrolling!

Stone carvings might last centuries, but they are heavy and difficult to move (especially if they are on a cave wall). Thousands of years ago, the search was on to find a writing material that was **LIGHTER** and so easier to carry.

FIVE ANCIENT WRITING MATERIALS

PAPYRUS
Made from a tall reed that grew near the Nile river in Egypt, these long strips were rolled into scrolls.
(Ancient Egypt, 2900 BCE)

SILK
This was light and smooth, perfect for writing on.
(China, 700 BCE)

BAMBOO
Thin strips of bamboo were sewn together and used to make scrolls.
(China, 400 BCE)

PARCHMENT
Made from animal skin that was soaked, stretched, scraped and smoothed, this was first turned into scrolls and, later, books.
(Ancient Greece, 200 BCE)

TRUE OR FALSE?

Red ink used to be made from squashed insects.

TRUE!

Red ink used to get its vibrant colour from the cochineal insect. These insects were scraped from the cactus leaves on which they lived. Next, they were dried and pummelled into a powder. When mixed with aluminium, this made cochineal – a type of bright red dye.

It was also made from soot and glue!

DID YOU KNOW...?

In 105 CE, Chinese inventor, **Cai Lun,** combined wood pulp with water and smoothed it onto cloth. The mixture dried to create ... **paper**!

The invention of paper changed everything. Paper was more **lightweight** than parchment and **cheaper** to produce, too. It became much **easier** for more and more people to spread knowledge and to communicate with each other.

Get Printing!

In the ninth century, it may have taken 75 years to create the world-famous Book of Kells.

Long ago, every book was **WRITTEN** and illustrated by hand. It could take a year or more to make a single copy. Then, in 1436, German inventor Johannes Gutenberg built a printing press that could produce 250 pages an hour!

FIVE BONUSES OF GUTENBERG'S PRINTING PRESS

1. Metal letters could easily be moved and reused, which made printing faster.

2. Because printing was much faster than handwriting, it was cheaper!

3. It wasn't just rich people who could afford to buy books now.

4. More and more people learned to read.

5. It became easier to spread ideas and knowledge around the world.

TRUE OR FALSE?

About 600 new books are published around the world every day!

FALSE!

UNESCO (the United Nations Educational, Scientific and Cultural Organization) estimates that the real answer is around **6,000** books a day. (But don't worry. You don't have to read all of them.)

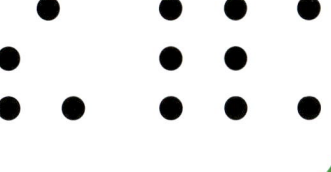

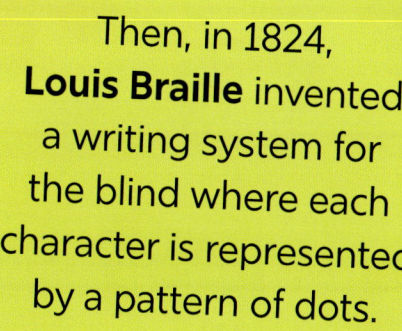

DID YOU KNOW...?

Two French men made a great difference to visually impaired readers worldwide. In 1786, **Valentin Haüy** – who founded the first school for the blind in Paris – printed a book with **raised letters** that could be read by touch.

Then, in 1824, **Louis Braille** invented a writing system for the blind where each character is represented by a pattern of dots.

Braille books are still printed and read all over the world today.

GET SIGNALLING!

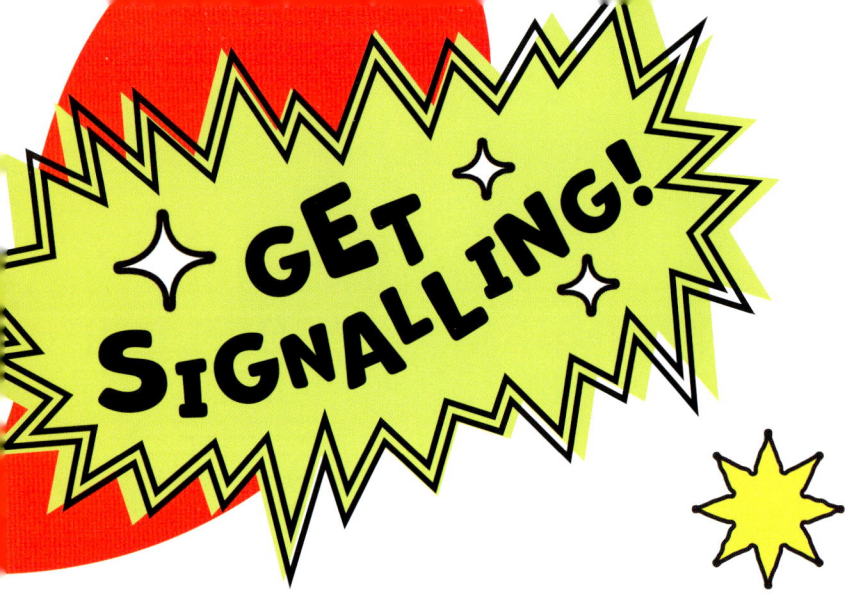

Long ago, there was no postal service, no telephone network and definitely no internet. But people could communicate using **SIGHT** or **SOUND**. Sometimes, they still do!

TRUE OR FALSE?

If you have two small flags, you can use them to say absolutely anything.

TRUE!

Semaphore is a type of signalling that uses flags to represent letters and numbers. By using these flag positions, you can communicate any message you like!

This word comes from the ancient Greek words meaning 'sign' and 'bearer'.

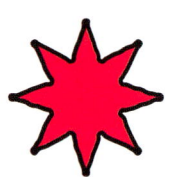

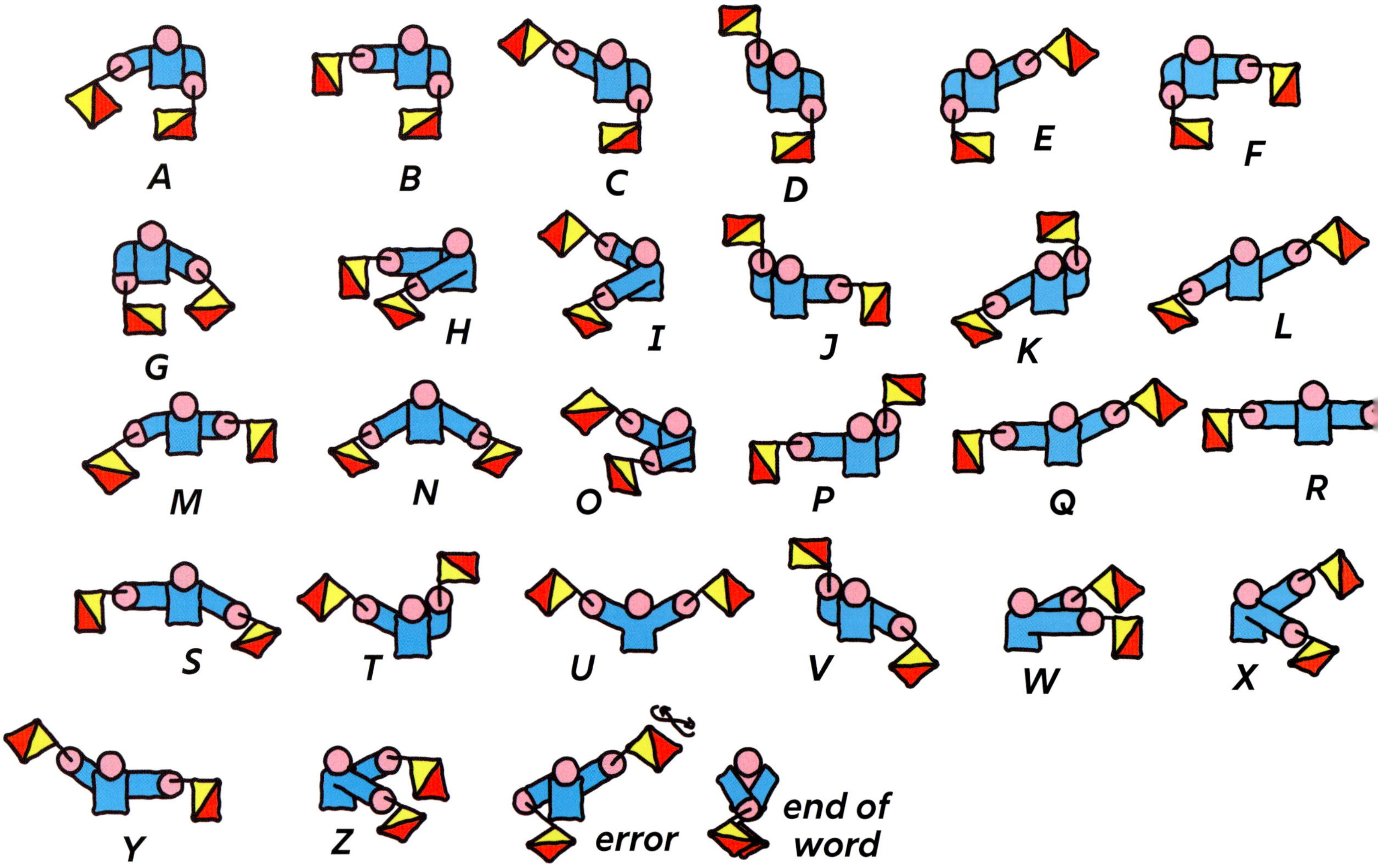

DID YOU KNOW...?

Around the world, the colours of traffic lights are always red, amber and green. Sometimes, there may be small differences in shade; sometimes, lights are displayed horizontally instead of vertically. But **red** always means **STOP** and **green** always means **GO**.

The same colours are used on the railways, too!

So, wherever you go, you can always be sure what traffic lights and pedestrian lights mean.

THREE TYPES OF SIGNAL

SMOKE
The only equipment needed to create a smoke signal is a fire; in ancient China, smoke signals were used to show that the enemy was on the way.

CANNON FIRE
The sound of cannonball fire can travel a few kilometres; during Ramadan, it is traditional in some countries to fire a cannon at sunset, to signal the start of prayers and the end of fasting.

DRUMMING
In parts of West Africa, drums are used to send messages; the drumming mimics sounds made in speech!

GET INVENTING!

In 1837, the electric telegraph made it possible to send **LONG-DISTANCE** messages by whizzing electrical signals along a wire. One of its inventors, Samuel Morse, developed a code to go with the new telegraph. Morse Code was made up of dots (these were sent as short electrical signals) and dashes (long electrical signals).

MORSE CODE

If you'd like to communicate using Morse Code, here it is!

A	•—	N	—•
B	—•••	O	———
C	—•—•	P	•——•
D	—••	Q	——•—
E	•	R	•—•
F	••—•	S	•••
G	——•	T	—
H	••••	U	••—
I	••	V	•••—
J	•———	W	•——
K	—•—	X	—••—
L	•—••	Y	—•——
M	——	Z	——••

DID YOU KNOW...?

There are **more** mobile phones in the world than people.

FOUR MORE INVENTIONS

TELEPHONE
Invented by Alexander Graham Bell in 1876, this allowed people to communicate instantly across long distancesa!

RADIO
Both Nikola Tesla and Guglielmo Marconi were involved with the invention of the radio. Marconi sent and received the first radio messages in 1896.

TRANSATLANTIC COMMUNICATION
In 1956, the first telephone call across the Atlantic Ocean was made using two cables laid along the seabed and joined in the middle.

Amazingly, this wasn't the first transatlantic cable! Queen Victoria and US president James Buchanan sent telegraph messages to each other along the first cable in 1858!

TRUE OR FALSE?

In Morse Code, SOS stands for SAVE OUR SOULS.

(MOSTLY) FALSE!

The international distress signal SOS was chosen simply because the letters were easy to remember: S (dot, dot, dot), O (dash, dash, dash), S (dot, dot, dot). It was only later that the phrase Save Our Souls was invented, simply because it matched the letters ... and it made sense!

GET BROADCASTING!

You might think that **RADIOS** are old-fashioned. But even though they were discovered over a century ago, radio waves are still the easiest way of informing, entertaining and communicating with huge numbers of people, **INSTANTLY**.

Radio waves travel at the speed of light! As that's 300 million metres per second, this means radio broadcasting is VERY fast indeed.

DID YOU KNOW...?

If disaster strikes, emergency broadcasts are sent via radio because this is the most **reliable** network.

Radio waves can travel **thousands of kilometres**, away from a radio transmitter so, wherever you are in the world, you're likely to be within reach of a news broadcast.

TRUE OR FALSE?

Television is more popular than radio.

FALSE!

It's the other way round! Radios are cheap and easy to find, so more people are likely to own one. They are more portable than a television and can be powered by electricity or battery or even by winding them up! In the USA, more people listen to the radio each week than watch television. In parts of Africa, where radio broadcasts are available in more languages than television programmes, the same is true.

TYPES OF VERY USEFUL RADIO BROADCAST

LISTEN AND LEARN
Lessons can be broadcast on the radio when it's difficult for children to go to school.

MUSIC OF ALL KINDS
Radio stations pay to play music, but it's free for listeners.

NEWS FROM NEAR AND FAR
News bulletins tell us what's going on.

SPORTS COMMENTARIES
Many sporting events are not shown on the television or are pay-per-view, but these can often be heard on the radio instead.

WEATHER FORECASTS
Countries around the world give radio alerts if extreme weather is on the way.

GET INTO SPACE!

Many parts of our planet bristle with **COMMUNICATIONS INFRASTRUCTURE** – the equipment that's needed to send a message from one person to another. But if you're in the middle of a remote forest, there's less likely to be a fibre-optic cable for your message to travel along. Communications satellite technology was developed so everyone could stay in touch!

TRUE OR FALSE?

One of the reasons we have communications satellites is because our planet is shaped like a ball.

TRUE!

Earth's surface is curved. So if a signal were sent a very long way around the world, it would have to bend to reach its destination. Instead, signals are sent up to a communications satellite, before bouncing back down to another part of our planet.

Signals travel in two straight lines, like a ball that bounces off the side of a snooker table.

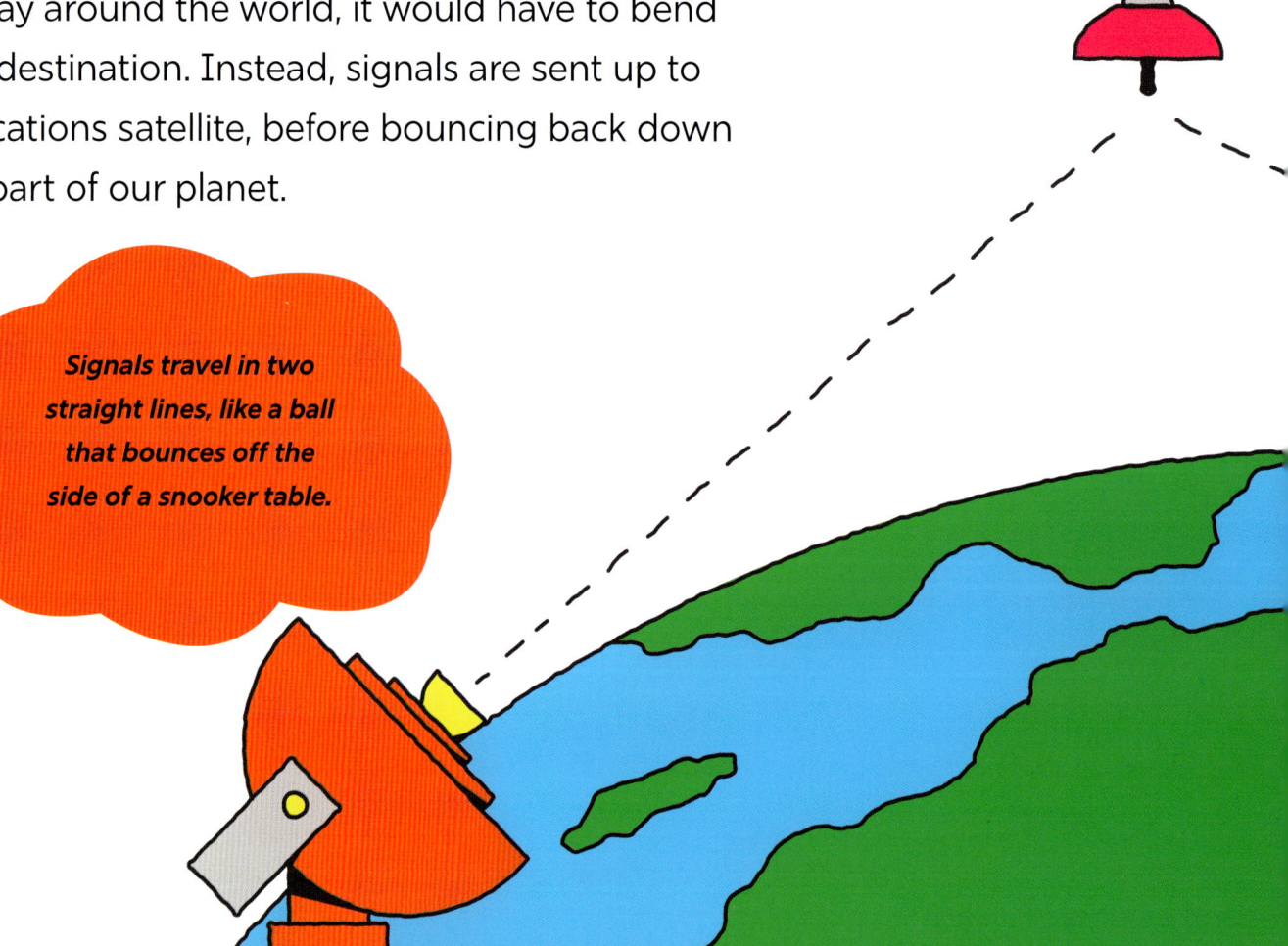

FOUR FACTS ABOUT SATELLITES

1. The first communications satellite was launched in 1962. It was called TELSTAR 1 and worked for 7 months!

2. GEOSYNCHRONOUS orbit means that satellites orbit Earth at the same rate as our planet spins.

3. There are over 3,000 communications satellites in space right now!

4. The time it takes for a signal to travel from Earth to a satellite and back down to Earth is ... less than a quarter of a second!

DID YOU KNOW...?

Interstellar radio messages (IRMs) are messages sent from our planet into space, in the hope of making contact with extra-terrestrial beings.

As radio waves travel at the **speed of light**, they go a lot faster than a spacecraft ... and they are cheaper to send, too!

GET ONLINE!

Did you know that before **1989** there were no websites and definitely no online shopping? Hardly anyone used email. Now, two-thirds of the world's population is online!

That's when top computer scientist Sir Tim Berners-Lee invented the World Wide Web.

THINGS PEOPLE DO ONLINE

- Talk to family on the other side of the world
- Order a takeaway
- Find out the weather forecast
- Book a flight
- Discover how to build a radio

A trillion other things – how many can YOU think of?

However, 2.6 billion people around the world are **not** online. For many, especially in developing countries, an internet connection is too expensive. Some do not have access to electricity. Others can't read or do not have the skills to get online.

TRUE OR FALSE?

The internet and the World Wide Web are the same thing.

FALSE!

They are totally different. The internet is the network of computers linked around our planet. But the World Wide Web is the extraordinarily huge collection of websites that everyone can visit, by using the internet.

Imagine the **INTERNET** is a busy road. The **WORLD WIDE WEB** is the shops and services along that road!

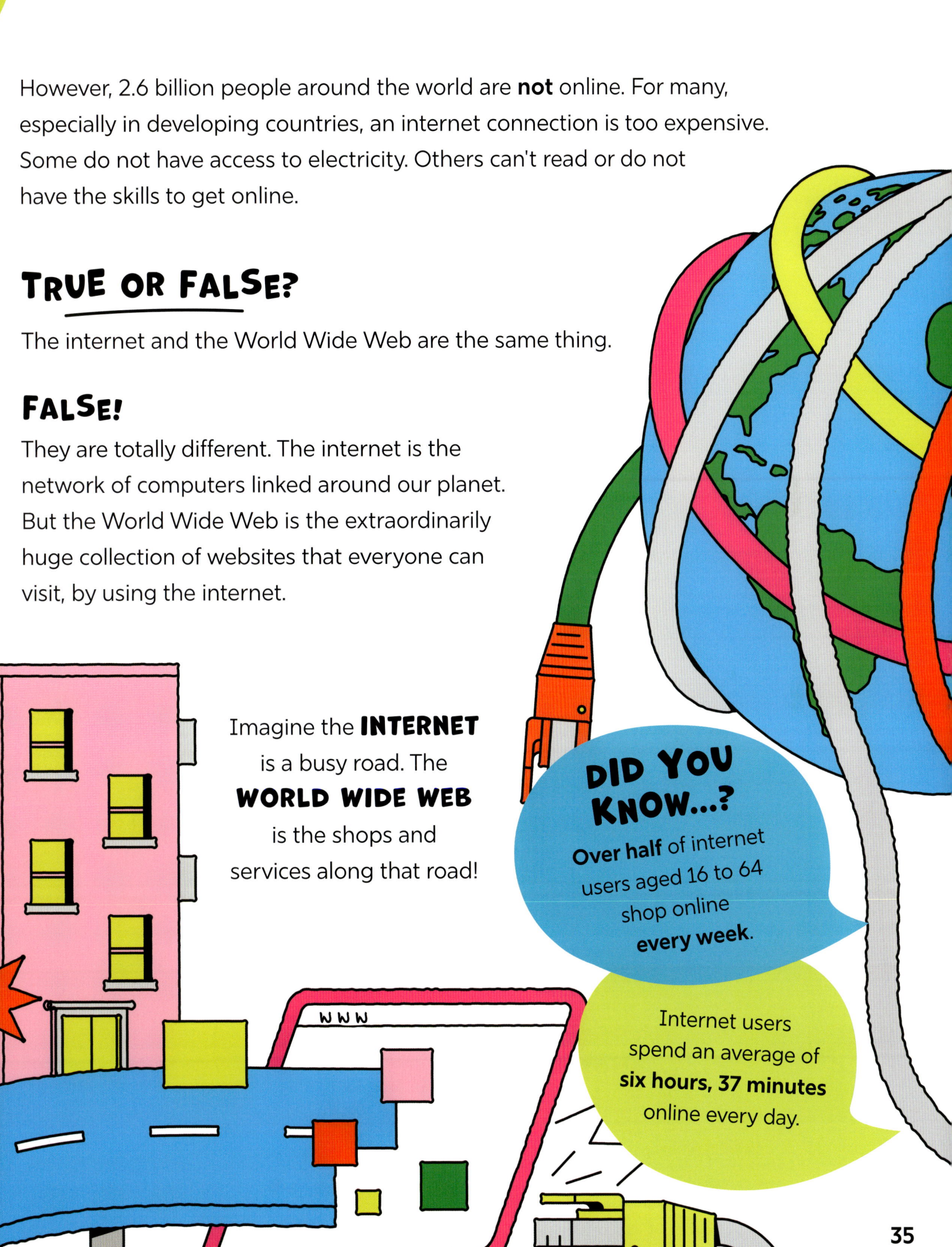

DID YOU KNOW...?

Over half of internet users aged 16 to 64 shop online **every week**.

Internet users spend an average of **six hours, 37 minutes** online every day.

GET SHARING!

Social media are different apps and websites that we use to **CONNECT** with others.

You need a device such as a mobile phone, a tablet or a computer to use social media!

THREE THINGS PEOPLE DO ON SOCIAL MEDIA

'LIKE' THINGS
This might mean clicking a thumbs-up or heart icon to show that they think something is great!

'SHARE' THINGS
When someone really admires a post, they might show it to their own followers too; they're not stealing the post because it's obvious that someone else created it.

SEARCH FOR 'CATS'
Funny cat videos are one of the most popular things on social media!

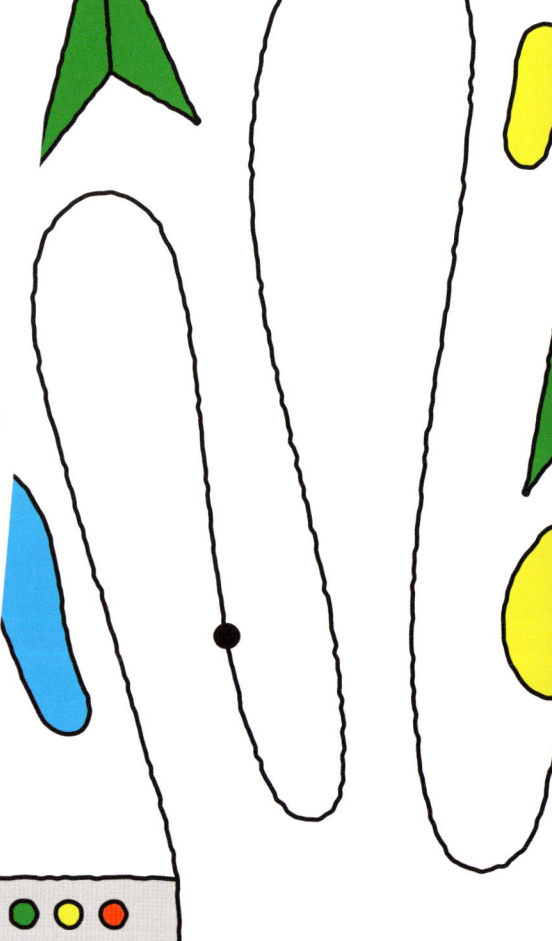

True or False?

A quarter of the world's population uses social media.

False!

In 2023, nearly two-thirds of the world's population used social media.

Did You Know...?

There are **age restrictions** for most social media platforms. For many, you need to be **13** years old to use them and for some, the age limit is **16** years old.

The reason for this is not to spoil your fun. It's because there can be unsuitable content online. By waiting until you're a little older to use social media, it makes it easier for you to recognise harmful posts and avoid them. Grown-ups aren't being unfair by making you wait until you're older to use social media; they're just trying to keep you safe.

GET CONVERSING!

If you're ever sad, worried or upset about something, the best thing to do is talk about it with someone. **SHARING** a problem can often help you to feel much, much better. Sometimes it's easier to talk to someone you don't live with, like a grandparent or cousin. Or you could chat to a friend. But don't forget that you can also talk to a teacher. They can be really good listeners.

They might also be able to help!

TRUE OR FALSE?

A conversation with a friend every day can boost your mood.

TRUE!

Research shows that chatting with a friend once a day can improve your mental health. Even if you're just cracking jokes, it counts. And it's not limited to one conversation. You can have as many as you like! The important thing is to connect with someone.

DID YOU KNOW...?

The saying 'a problem shared is a problem halved' is about a **hundred** years old.

It means that if you tell someone what's worrying you, the problem is **shared** between two people. So it's half as big!

FIVE REASONS WHY CONVERSATIONS ARE A GREAT IDEA

1. They make friendships stronger.

2. Talking is better than keeping worries to yourself.

3. Problems might not seem so bad when you say them out loud.

4. If others know what's wrong, they may be able to help.

5. Sharing worries helps to relieve stress.

GET CHATTING!

If you've just moved house or started a new school or club, kicking off a conversation with a total stranger is probably the last thing you feel like doing. But take a deep breath and have a go. You might be surprised at how easy it is to make friends.

FIVE CONVERSATION STARTERS (AT A NEW SCHOOL)

1. Ask someone what they think of the school and what the best bits are!
2. Tell someone they look amazing.
3. Say something super nice about the school or its pupils.
4. Ask someone about themselves.
5. If someone is struggling to open a door or carry seventeen boxes all on their own, offer to help!

Most people LOVE to talk about themselves!

TRUE OR FALSE?

Talking sticks were used by Native American tribes to make sure that nobody interrupted during meetings.

TRUE!

A person was only allowed to speak when they were holding the talking stick – sometimes known as a speaker's staff. This way, everyone had a chance to speak.

DID YOU KNOW...? There are different types of **question.** Some encourage others to talk ... and some really don't!

A **close-ended question** is one that has only a few possible answers. If you start a conversation with one of these, then it could be over very quickly. For example ...

Do you like doughnuts?

Is your name Bernard?

An **open-ended question** might include the words **WHAT, WHEN, WHY, WHERE, WHO** and **HOW** and could have a variety of answers. It's an opportunity for someone to give a really thrilling answer and start a long conversation. For example ...

What's the best way of surviving an apocalypse?

If you were in charge of the world, what would you do?

GET SPEAKING OUT!

Communication doesn't always happen between just two people. Sometimes, one person communicates with a crowd, perhaps to explain something or simply to entertain them. When you make a speech to a large group, this is called **PUBLIC SPEAKING**.

FOUR TYPES OF PUBLIC SPEAKING

PRESENTATION
Whether it's in front of an auditorium full of people or in front of your class, this is a chance to inform and explain.

ACTING
Actors don't just have to speak in public, they often have to memorise their lines first; they can't just make the words up as they go along!

STAND-UP COMEDY
Comedians are public speakers, too; their aim is to entertain their audience ... and make them laugh!

POLITICAL SPEECH
This is when a politician tries to persuade a crowd that they are right!

DID YOU KNOW...?
On 28 August 1963 in Washington, DC, USA, **Martin Luther King, Jr.** gave his famous 'I Have A Dream' speech to a crowd of ... **a quarter of a million people.**

Millions more watched on television. The **civil-rights activist** called for equality. Over 60 years later, it remains one of the most **inspirational** speeches ever.

TRUE OR FALSE?

If you feel nervous before public speaking, your speech is guaranteed to be TERRIBLE.

FALSE!

It means nothing of the sort. If you're scared of public speaking, you're not alone. Even some of the greatest public speakers feel nervous about standing up in front of a crowd. But this does not mean that they will make a terrible job of it.
Did you know that some nerves are actually a good thing?! They show that you're experiencing an adrenalin rush, which can actually help you to perform better!

GET CONNECTED!

Getting connected with friends and family helps us to feel happy, valued and cared for ... whether we're in the same room, the next street, the next town, the next country, over the sea or on the other side of the world. Connecting doesn't just mean talking to people. Here are just a few of the many ways you can **STAY IN TOUCH**.

10 WAYS TO CONNECT WITH OTHERS

1. Take part in a school play or quiz.
2. Play games with friends.
3. Learn another language.
4. Listen to the radio.
5. Play in an orchestra.
6. Send a letter.
7. Share a worry.
8. Learn sign language.
9. Tell a joke.
10. Visit someone.

DID YOU KNOW...?
Neuroscientist Matthew Lieberman says that human brains are actually wired to **connect with others**.

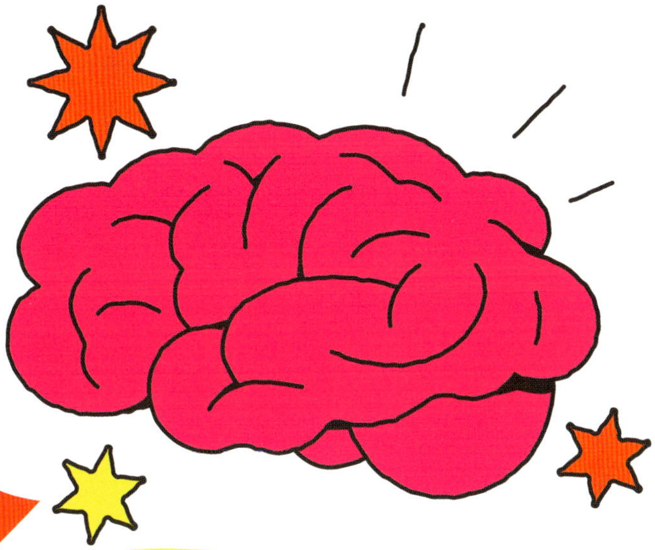

Just as the brain reacts to physical things, such as eating a delicious ice cream or breaking a leg, it reacts **just as strongly** – and sometimes more so – to pleasurable or painful events that involve other **people**.

How amazing is that?!

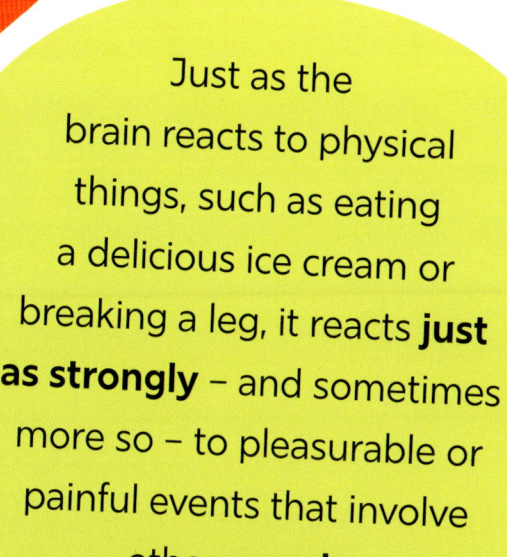

TRUE OR FALSE?

Staying connected helps us to feel happier.

TRUE!

Research has shown that connecting with others helps us to be happier. But that's not all. Amazingly, it helps us to be healthier, too. Human connection can actually strengthen our immune systems, so we're better able to fight illness.

GLOSSARY

adrenalin rush a burst of energy

apocalypse a horribly destructive event

body language when you move your body in a way that tells others what you mean

civil-rights activist someone who campaigns for everyone to have equal rights

communication when information is shared

connect link up

cuneiform an ancient way of writing

decipher to decode something; to work out what it means

demotic language used by ordinary people

expression a particular way your face moves to show emotion, such as raising eyebrows to show surprise

gesture when you move parts of your body to show what you mean; for example, a nod is another way of saying 'yes'

hieroglyphics an ancient Egyptian written language that used symbols instead of words

larynx the part of your throat used for breathing, swallowing and talking

lungs organs in your chest that supply your body with oxygen

lyrics the words to songs

neuroscientist a scientist who studies the brain and nervous system

playwright someone who writes plays

printing press a machine invented in 1436 that prints pages with words and pictures

pulp when something is wet and mushy

pummelled bashed over and over again

satellite an object in space that travels around a larger object

species a group of living things that look alike and can reproduce, such as lions, humans or roses

Sumerians people who lived in Iraq between four and six thousand years ago

tactile using touch

transatlantic something that crosses from one side of the Atlantic Ocean to the other

vocal cords folds of stretchy tissue that create sound when you speak

FURTHER INFORMATION

BOOKS

A Problem Shared: Talking about Mental Health by Louise Spilsbury (Franklin Watts, 2020)

Confident Kids: Keep Safe by Honor Head and Jennifer Jamieson (Franklin Watts, 2024)

Super Tech: Space by Clive Gifford (Wayland, 2024)

The History of the Computer by Rachel Ignotofsky (Wren & Rook, 2022)

Think Big: The Greatest Ideas in Technology by Sonya Newland (Wayland, 2022)

PLACES TO VISIT

If you'd like to see the Rosetta Stone (see page 37) and find out about hieroglyphs and ancient languages, visit The British Museum in London, UK.

www.britishmuseum.org/

An Enigma machine is on display at The National Museum of Computing in Bletchley Park, Milton Keynes, UK. There's lots more information about the amazing mathematicians who cracked the Enigma code, too.

www.tnmoc.org/

Find out about the history of information technology at the Museum of Communication in Burntisland near Edinburgh, UK.

https://museumofcommunication.org.uk/

INDEX

ancient Egyptians 16–17, 19, 22
ancient Greeks 19, 26
animal communication 14–15

Bell, Alexander Graham 29
Berners-Lee, Sir Tim 34
body language 4, 10–11
books 14, 18, 19, 22, 24, 25
Braille 13, 25
Braille, Louis 25

code-breaking 19, 21

Gutenberg, Johannes 24

Haüy, Valentin 25
hieroglyphics/hieroglyphs 16–17, 19

indigenous communication 8, 41
internet 26, 34–35
inventions, communication 28–29

Keller, Helen 13
King, Jr., Martin Luther 42

languages 8–9, 19, 20, 21, 31, 44
letters 12, 20, 21, 24, 25, 26, 29
Lieberman, Matthew 45
listening 5, 11, 31, 38, 44
Lun, Cai 23

Marconi, Guglielmo 29
mental health 37, 38, 39, 45

Morse Code 28, 29
Morse, Samuel 28

paper 22, 23
petroglyphs 16
phrases 9, 11, 38
pictographs 16
printing 24–25
public speaking 42–43

Queen Victoria 29

radio 29, 30–31, 33, 34, 44
radio waves 30, 33
Rosetta Stone 19

satellites 32–33
senses 12, 13, 26
Shakespeare, William 9
signals 26–27
 semaphore 26
sign-language 11, 12, 13, 45
social media 36–37
sounds 6, 7, 8, 11, 16, 18, 20, 21, 26, 27
Sumerians 18

telephones 26, 28, 29, 36
Tesla, Nikola 29

websites 34–36